ESSENTIAL LIBRARY OF THE
INFORMATION AGE

CONTENT OWNERSHIP AND COPYRIGHT

by Carolee Laine

CONTENT CONSULTANT
Brandy Karl
University Libraries' Copyright Officer
Pennsylvania State University

Essential Library

An Imprint of Abdo Publishing | abdopublishing.com

abdopublishing.com

Published by Abdo Publishing, a division of ABDO, PO Box 398166, Minneapolis, Minnesota 55439. Copyright © 2017 by Abdo Consulting Group, Inc. International copyrights reserved in all countries. No part of this book may be reproduced in any form without written permission from the publisher. Essential Library™ is a trademark and logo of Abdo Publishing.

Printed in the United States of America, North Mankato, Minnesota
052016
092016

THIS BOOK CONTAINS
RECYCLED MATERIALS

Cover Photo: Red Line Editorial
Interior Photos: Frank Micelotta/Invision/AP Images, 5; Nick Ut/AP Image, 7; Georgios Art/iStockphoto, 9; iStockphoto, 11; Bizuayehu Tesfaye/AP Images, 14; Nejron Photo/Shutterstock Images, 16; Purestock/Thinkstock, 19; Wavebreakmedia Ltd/Thinkstock, 20; Helga Esteb/Shutterstock Images, 25; Shutterstock Images, 27, 29, 47, 51, 54, 61, 71, 75, 79; Warner Bros./Everett Collection, 33; Tim Boyd/AP Images, 35; Jacquelyn Martin/AP Images, 37; Thinkstock, 39, 94; Public Domain, 41; Buena Vista Pictures/Everett Collection, 44; Joe Marquette/AP Images, 49; Landmark Media/Shutterstock Images, 56; Layland Masuda/Shutterstock Images, 59; Highwaystarz-Photography/iStockphoto, 64; Thinkstock Images/Stockbyte/Thinkstock, 66; Justin Sullivan/Getty Images, 69; John Greim/LightRocket/Getty Images, 81; PHOTOS.com/Thinkstock, 84; Dominic Favre/Keystone/AP Images, 87; Laurent Gillieron/Keystone/AP Images, 89; Everett Collection, 91; Yury Ryzhov/Hemera/Thinkstock, 93; Alexandra Wyman/Invision for IFTA/AP Images, 99

Editor: Angela Wiechmann
Series Designer: Craig Hinton

Publisher's Cataloging in Publication Data

Names: Laine, Carolee, author.
Title: Content ownership and copyright / by Carolee Laine.
Description: Minneapolis, MN : Abdo Publishing, [2017] | Series: Essential library
    of the information age | Includes bibliographical references and index.
Identifiers: LCCN 2015960303 | ISBN 9781680782844 (lib. bdg.) |
    ISBN 9781680774733 (ebook)
Subjects: LCSH: Bibliographical citations--Juvenile literature. | Copyright--
    Juvenile literature. | Public domain (Copyright law)--Juvenile literature.
Classification: DDC 346.04--dc23
LC record available at http://lccn.loc.gov/2015960303

CONTENTS

CHAPTER 1

4 Protecting
   Creative Efforts

CHAPTER 2

18 How Copyright Works

CHAPTER 3

28 Using
    Copyrighted Material

CHAPTER 4

40 Public Domain

CHAPTER 5

50 Intellectual Property

CHAPTER 6

58 Copyrights and Schools

CHAPTER 7

68 Copyrights in the
    Digital Age

CHAPTER 8

80 Global Copyright Issues

CHAPTER 9

90 What's Wrong
    with Copyrights?

100 Essential Facts
102 Glossary
104 Additional Resources
106 Source Notes
110 Index
112 About the Author
112 About the Consultant

CHAPTER 1

PROTECTING CREATIVE EFFORTS

Marvin Gaye was a legendary singer and songwriter in the 1960s and 1970s. Many of his hits remained popular for decades. In 1977, Gaye wrote and produced "Got to Give It Up," which hit Number 1 on American charts. Years later, in 2015, the song gained renewed media interest when it became part of a federal court case.

Many people found the 2013 hit song "Blurred Lines" controversial because of its subject matter and video. But from a legal standpoint, the song was controversial because of its musical similarity to Gaye's "Got to Give It Up." Singer Robin Thicke and songwriter Pharrell Williams claimed Gaye's work had inspired their song. Thicke recalled telling Williams, "We should make something like that, something with that groove."[1]

Gaye's children, who had inherited rights to his songs after his death in 1984, threatened legal action against Thicke and Williams for copyright infringement. Copyright infringement

"Blurred Lines" by Pharrell Williams, *left*, and Robin Thicke, *right*, led many to question the line between inspiration and infringement.

CONSEQUENCES OF "BLURRED LINES"

The $7.4-million-dollar settlement in the "Blurred Lines" case was one of the largest of its kind, but that was not the most important issue to many people in the music industry. The larger issue was what might happen as a consequence of the ruling against Thicke and Williams. Some critics of the verdict argued that most popular songs rely on borrowed sounds and elements from other songs. They pointed out that sometimes innovation depends on creative copying. They expressed concern that the verdict might limit creativity in music by preventing new songs from referencing older classics. As Williams commented, "The verdict handicaps any creator out there who is making something that might be inspired by something else."[3]

occurs when people make unauthorized use of material protected by copyright. In turn, Thicke and Williams sued Gaye's heirs, claiming their song was different from "Got to Give It Up."

A US district court heard the case. Jurors were instructed to compare the songs only on the basis of their sheet music versions. The jury determined "Blurred Lines" infringed on the copyright to Gaye's music but that Thicke and Williams had not willfully, or intentionally, copied Gaye's song. The jury awarded Gaye's children nearly $7.4 million.[2]

Legal experts and many musicians felt the verdict confused inspiration for infringement. They argued that although elements of a musical composition are protected by copyright, a general style—a "groove," as Thicke put it—is not.

Marvin Gaye's family stood by their belief that "Blurred Lines" infringed on the late singer's copyrighted work.

The case reveals that US copyright laws are extremely complex. Some people feel the laws are necessary to protect content ownership and promote the progress of human knowledge. Other people feel the laws hinder creativity rather than encourage it.

THE PURPOSE OF COPYRIGHTS

As established in Article I, Section 8 of the US Constitution, copyright law protects creative efforts in order to encourage the growth of human knowledge. Copyrights give the creators of intellectual and artistic works exclusive rights, for a limited time, that allow them to control how their works are used.

George Washington signed the first US copyright law in 1790. Over the years, the law has been revised several times. The last major revision of copyright law took place in 1976, with several smaller revisions since then. The changes have broadened the scope of copyright, changed the duration of copyright protection, and addressed new technologies that complicated the existing copyright laws.

All forms of original creative expression are eligible for copyright protection, as long as they can be written on paper, recorded, painted, sculpted, put into a computer, or created in some other permanent format. This includes literary works; musical works; dramatic works; pantomimes and choreographic works; pictorial, graphic, and sculptural works; motion pictures and other audiovisual works; sound recordings; and architectural works.

> **"** If you can see it, read it, watch it, or hear it—with or without the use of a computer, projector, or other machine—the work is likely eligible for copyright protection. **"** [4]
>
> —Kenneth Crews, copyright scholar

US copyright law dates back to 1790, when George Washington signed the first such law into effect.

GIRL SCOUTS AND THE FREEDOM TO SING SONGS

Copyright infringement of musical works can be a costly mistake, as the "Blurred Lines" case proved. In 1996, even the Girl Scouts were targeted for what at first seemed to be a costly infringement.

According to US copyright law, songwriters can collect royalties when their copyrighted works are used in public performances. On behalf of its members, the American Society of Composers, Authors and Publishers (ASCAP) collects royalties from users such as radio stations, restaurants, and dance clubs. Each company pays from a few hundred dollars to several thousand dollars a year for the right to use copyrighted songs.

In 1995, ASCAP informed the American Camping Association that it would have to pay a licensing fee for any copyrighted music performed at its more than 2,000 camps nationwide. That included music performed by Girl Scouts staying at American Camping Association sites.

Singing songs around a campfire is a tradition for Girl Scouts. But many Girl Scout groups could not afford the licensing fees, so

Campfire sing-alongs were a Girl Scout tradition—until copyrights got involved.

they had to eliminate copyrighted music from their sing-alongs. In the resulting 1996 media storm, news programs featured sad video of Girl Scouts performing the Macarena—the year's biggest dance craze—without music. And newspapers featured stories about bans on such campfire favorites as "Puff the Magic Dragon" and "This Land Is Your Land."

In view of the negative publicity, ASCAP backed down, saying it had only meant to charge professional musicians performing at large resorts. The organization agreed to return any fees it had collected from Girl Scout camps.

FEDERAL EMPLOYEE EXCEPTIONS

The first copyright law in the United States was signed into effect by President Washington. But today, the president's official work cannot be copyrighted. Works created by officers or employees of the federal government are not entitled to US copyright protection. That includes material created by the most famous federal employee of them all—the president.

Under this exception, works such as presidential inaugural speeches and state of the union addresses are not copyrightable. A photograph of the president delivering a speech may be copyrighted, so long as the photographer is not a federal employee. In fact, works by the official White House photographer are not protected by copyright. Anyone, including students, may freely use those photographs.

However, not everything created by US government officers or employees automatically falls under this exception. Works created outside official duties, such as personal letters or journals, are copyrightable by the creators.

An idea or a fact cannot be protected by copyright. Rather, the particular expression of the idea or fact can be. For example, an author can write a biography about George Washington. The author does not control exclusive rights to the facts about Washington's life, however. Other authors are free to write about Washington using the same facts. What is protected is each author's words—the unique expression of the common facts. Also, to be eligible for copyright, a work must be at least minimally creative. For example, phone books or lists of common facts do not qualify for copyright protection. In addition, copyrights protect original works, not those copied from another source. In some cases, a copyright protects a work that was created by adding to or transforming previously created material. But as the case of

"Blurred Lines" indicates, transforming copyrighted material can be a complicated legal matter.

COPYRIGHT AND CONSUMERS

Musicians, authors, and other creators are not the only ones who need to understand copyright laws. The laws also affect everyday individuals who come into contact with the creative works the copyright holders offer to the public. Copyright determines how people read, watch, and listen to works of creative expression. It especially dictates how they use and share the material. In some cases, not understanding or following copyright law can make the difference between legal and illegal activity.

Joel Tenenbaum was a college student at Boston University when his music-downloading habits gained national attention in the early 2000s. Over a period of several years, Tenenbaum illegally downloaded and distributed thousands of songs. The music was protected by copyright, and he did not pay to download it.

Tenenbaum realized his actions were illegal. He chose to ignore warning letters from record companies informing him of the illegal use of copyrighted material. Then, in 2007, four record companies sued Tenenbaum for 30 counts of copyright infringement. The cases corresponded to 30 specific songs he had downloaded.[5]

Two years later, a federal jury found him guilty. He was ordered to pay the record companies $22,500 for each song. The total came to $675,000. Later, the judge reduced the amount to $67,500, but the record companies appealed the decision.[6] A circuit court

of appeals upheld the original decision and awarded the record companies the full amount.

Even though he lost the appeal, the outcome could have been much worse for Tenenbaum. Under federal law, the court could have awarded the record companies $4.5 million. Rather, Tenenbaum had to pay only 15 percent of that maximum amount.[7]

Tenenbaum's supporters argued that millions of people downloaded songs without paying, via popular free file-sharing websites. Tenenbaum just happened to be the unlucky person who got caught. They claimed the fines had been set high in order

In a landmark case, Joel Tenenbaum was accused of infringement after illegally downloading thousands of songs from file-sharing sites.

to make an example of him. The record companies seemed to be sending a message to all those who were illegally downloading copyrighted material. Some supporters complained that the record companies were getting rich by requiring fees for music that should be freely shared. They likened it to sharing a CD with friends and family.

On the other side, those who supported the legal decision pointed out that copyright infringement affects more than record companies. It also impacts recording artists, songwriters, musicians, technicians, and many other people who depend on the sale of recordings for their income. Some groups, such as the Motion Picture Association of America, liken the illegal use of copyrighted material to stealing.

Tenenbaum's case illustrates two important issues about copyrights. One, they protect content ownership. And two, violating copyright law can result in a great personal cost—even if millions of other people are guilty of the same infringement. Avoiding infringement is one important reason to understand how copyright works.

Copyright infringement of music affects the income of musicians, producers, and many others in the industry.

CHAPTER 2

HOW COPYRIGHT WORKS

Copyright protection begins automatically as soon as a creator puts a work into permanent form. For example, an author's original words are protected as soon as they are written on paper, typed into a computer, or dictated into a recording device. Copyright protection applies to young people as well. A student owns the copyright to a story she writes for an assignment or a painting he creates for art class.

The work does not need to be distributed, shared, or published in any way in order for the copyright to apply. That said, publication is an important concept in copyright law. Knowing whether or when a work has been published is key to determining certain rights, such as how long copyright protection will last. For copyright purposes, a work is considered published when copies are sold, rented, lent, given away, or made available to the public with the copyright owner's permission. Even if no copies are ultimately sold or distributed, a work is considered published if copies are available.

The moment words are written in permanent form, copyright goes into effect.

COPYRIGHT NOTICE AND REGISTRATION

When works are distributed in any way, many creators include copyright notices to visually inform the public the work is protected. The copyright symbol, consisting of the letter *C* with a circle around it, is the official mark of copyright protection described in US copyright law. A full copyright notice includes either the symbol, the word *copyright*, or the abbreviation *copr*. A notice also includes the date the work was published and the name of the copyright owner. For example, © 2016 Mary Smith.

> " At the moment, everyone gets a copyright as soon as the work is written down or otherwise fixed, whether they want one or not. " [1]
>
> —James Boyle, *The Public Domain: Enclosing the Commons of the Mind*

Prior to March 1989, all works required such a copyright notice in order to be protected. Omitting the notice on a work first published before March 1989 could have resulted in the loss of copyright protection. Now the use of a copyright notice is optional but still recommended. The notice serves as added security for copyright owners and an extra warning to potential users.

As a further step, a creator may register a copyright in the Copyright Office of the Library of Congress for a minimal fee. Just as with copyright notices, registration is recommended but not required. Registration provides special benefits. For example, if a creator needs to defend a copyright, having the copyright

For copyright purposes, a work is considered published when the creator makes it available to the public.

registered makes the complicated legal process a bit easier to initiate.

EXCLUSIVE RIGHTS

Registered or not, copyrights provide creators with exclusive rights for a limited time. In most cases, that means the copyright owner alone controls the first use and/or sale of the work for a certain number of years. At the time of the owner's death, the copyright passes to that person's heirs. Authors, artists, and musicians may wish to transfer their rights to publishers or record companies, which may be better able to develop and market the works. In return for a copyright transfer, the creators or their heirs may receive royalties, which are shares of the money generated by sales.

In most cases, copyright owners have exclusive rights to reproduce their work in copies. Examples include making photocopies of a story; digitizing a photograph; or creating a phonorecord, such as an audiobook, of a novel. Copyright owners can distribute copies of their work to

REGISTERING COPYRIGHT

Creators register copyrights with the US Copyright Office. Online application is preferred for literary works, visual arts, performing arts, movies, and sound recordings. An application consists of a completed form, nonreturnable copies of the work, and a filing fee. After the application is processed, the Copyright Office issues a registration certificate. The registration is effective on the date the Copyright Office received all required materials and fees for the application, regardless of how long it took to process and mail the certificate.

WORK FOR HIRE

In most cases, the creator of a work is the copyright owner. However, copyright law also covers two categories of works made for hire, for which the creator does not own the copyright. One category consists of employees who create works for their employers. Examples include staff journalists who write articles for the newspaper that employs them and computer programmers who create software programs for their employers. Copyright ownership for these works belongs to the employers, not the creators.

Another category of work made for hire involves companies or individuals that commission independent contractors to create works. One example is a freelance artist hired to draw illustrations for a publishing company's book. A written agreement between the independent contractor and the company specifies that the work is made for hire. The artwork and copyright ownership belong to the publisher.

the public by sale, gift, rental, lease, or lending. Copyright owners control the rights to public performances and displays of literary, musical, and dramatic works as well as dances, pantomimes, movies, and other audiovisual works. Copyright owners also control the rights to public displays of pictures, graphics, and sculptures. In the case of sound recordings, copyright owners control the right to perform the work publicly via digital audio transmission, such as over the Internet.

In general, having exclusive control means copyright owners have the right to allow—or not allow—others to use their works in certain ways. For instance, copyright owners can allow or forbid the printing, recording, performance, translation, or adaptation of their work. When copyright owners do grant others permission to use their works, the owners are entitled to payments.

RIGHT TO PAYMENT

Copyright holders can refuse others' requests to use their works. For the 1997 movie *Titanic*, director James Cameron requested permission to feature a reproduction of a famous Picasso painting aboard the ship as it sinks. The Picasso estate owns the copyright to the original painting, which was never on the *Titanic*. Although the estate refused the permission request, Cameron featured the painting anyway.

The Artists Rights Society became involved. Finally, Cameron agreed to pay a fee to the Picasso estate. And then when a 3-D version of *Titanic* was released in 2012, the Artists Rights Society requested that Cameron pay another fee.

Critics questioned the fairness of having to pay for the right to show a painting in a movie—let alone paying again for a new release of the same movie. Others supported rights to payments, especially given that permission had been denied in the first place.

DERIVATIVE WORKS

Copyright owners can also create derivative works of their original works. These are new works—such as screenplays, translations, or musical arrangements—based on original works. Sometimes called an adaptation, a derivative work must include some or all of the original work, and it must add new, original copyrightable material. Examples of adaptations include movies based on plays or novels, sculptures based on drawings, drawings based on photographs, and revisions of websites. The copyright owner is the only person who has the right to create—or authorize others to create— derivative works. Other people may not produce derivative works of copyrighted material.

In 2015, the Batmobile became an important example of how derivative works fall under copyright protection. Mark Towle's

As Mark Towle learned, the Batmobile is a derivative work protected by the original work's copyright.

company created and sold Batmobile replicas. These cars looked like the Batmobiles from the 1966 *Batman* television series and the 1989 *Batman* movie.

DC Comics owned the rights to Batman products, though not specifically the rights to the 1966 series or 1989 movie. Nevertheless, DC Comics sued Towle for infringement. In the case *DC Comics v. Towle* (2015), the court ruled DC Comics' copyright extended to the Batmobile. The 1966 series and 1989 movie—and the Batmobile in general—were all considered derivative works

COPYRIGHT ACT OF 1976

The 1909 Copyright Act remained in effect for 68 years. During that time, changes in technology created a demand for revision of the law. In 1955, Congress authorized a program to analyze and revise copyright law to address new forms of communication, such as radio, television, photocopiers, and computers, as well as future changes. Then in 1961, the Copyright Office issued a report on the need for changes to the law.

The process of negotiation and compromise went on for 15 years. A copyright revision bill, passed by both houses of Congress and signed into law by President Gerald Ford in 1976, became effective on January 1, 1978. Register of Copyrights Barbara Ringer commented, "It is a source of wonder that somehow all of this succeeded in the end."[2]

The Copyright Act of 1976 addressed new forms of media and extended copyright protection to a wide range of creators and works. It clarified conditions for the use of copyrighted works and increased the duration of copyright protection for authors.

of the original copyrighted Batman material, which DC controlled. That meant Towle had no right to create derivative works such as the Batmobile replicas. Towle was guilty of infringement.

TERMS OF PROTECTION

Although copyright law grants exclusive rights to creators, those rights do not last forever. The original US Copyright Law of 1790 granted copyright protection for 14 years with an option for the creator to renew for another 14 years. The law has been revised several times since then to lengthen the duration of the protection. The Copyright Act of 1976 was an important reform. Today, the length of copyright protection varies, based on when the work was created.

Copyright terms vary, but a work published before 1923 is no longer protected in the United States.

Copyright protection for works created before 1923 has expired. A work created between 1923 and 1963 is protected by copyright for 95 years after its creation, if the original copyright was renewed during its expiration year. In contrast, a work published between 1964 and 1977 is protected for 95 years after its creation regardless of whether the original copyright was renewed. And a work created on or after January 1, 1978, is protected for at least 70 years after the author dies.

Copyright grants exclusive rights to the creator of a work, but there are exceptions. In certain situations, other people may use copyrighted material without permission. These situations fall under the principle of fair use.

CHAPTER 3

USING COPYRIGHTED MATERIAL

The best-selling Harry Potter series contains dozens of characters and specialized vocabulary from a fantasy world created by author J. K. Rowling. And the films based on the books expand on this fantasy world. Steven Vander Ark operated an extensive online Harry Potter reference guide. So he and RDR Books made plans to publish the *Harry Potter Lexicon* encyclopedia.

Rowling owned the copyrights to the seven books as well as two companion books. Warner Brothers Entertainment Inc. owned the rights to the entire film series. Rowling and Warner Brothers tried to block publication of the book. They claimed the *Harry Potter Lexicon* was copyright infringement, but RDR Books claimed it was fair use.

In *Warner Brothers Entertainment, Inc. v. RDR Books* (2008), the court ruled that Vander Ark's guide was not a fair use of the Harry Potter works. The court ordered RDR Books to pay damages of $6,750.[1] After the lawsuit, Vander Ark edited the book to avoid

J. K. Rowling took legal action when she felt another author infringed on her Harry Potter series.

infringement. *The Lexicon: An Unauthorized Guide to Harry Potter Fiction and Related Materials* was published in 2009.

On one hand, the judge indicated that reference guides to works of literature should be encouraged under copyright law. Reference guides help readers better understand and appreciate the original works. On the other hand, the judge stressed that reference guides must not copy extensively from original works without permission, as Vander Ark's book had done.

ALLOWING USE TO ADVANCE KNOWLEDGE

The *Harry Potter Lexicon* case reflects the complicated nature of fair use, infringement, and copyright law. The fair use law acknowledges the importance of allowing other people limited use of copyrighted material. To some extent, fair use limits copyright protection in order to advance knowledge and scholarship.

The Copyright Act of 1976 permits fair use of copyrighted materials for criticism, comment, news reporting, teaching, or research. Researchers' and students' work may depend on their ability to refer to or quote copyrighted material. As another example, the right to criticize a work, sometimes through humorous parody, depends on the ability to use elements of the

> ❝Copyright assures authors the right to their original expression, but encourages others to build freely upon the ideas and information conveyed by a work. . . . It is the means by which copyright advances the progress of science and art.❞[2]
>
> —Justice Sandra Day O'Connor, 1991

A parody is a work that ridicules an existing work by imitating it in a comic way. The parody uses some elements of the existing work to create a new work that, at least in part, comments on the original. One example of a parody is a song that uses the melody of an existing song but changes the lyrics in a humorous way. The new lyrics target the message or meaning of the original lyrics. Other forms of parody include comedy skits and movie spoofs.

Generally, a parody will be protected under fair use if it meets proper qualifications. In the case of a song parody, it must change the words for the purpose of commenting on the original work. Simply using an existing melody with different words does not qualify as a parody. Rather, it could be an infringement if the original song is copyrighted.

original material. Use of work outside of these conditions requires the user to seek permission from the copyright holder.

INFRINGEMENT AND THE LEGAL PROCESS

According to fair use guidelines, copyright owners give automatic consent to fair use of their work. However, copyright owners have the right to take legal action if they believe someone has gone beyond fair use. When owners believe their copyrights have been infringed, they can send cease and desist letters demanding infringers to stop the copyright violations. If the infringement continues, the copyright owner may wish to take legal action, such as a lawsuit. In these situations, courts have several options under the law.

If a copyright was not registered, the copyright owner who wins a lawsuit can collect the actual costs. This includes the owner's lost profits plus the infringer's gained profits.

The court may also award court costs and attorney fees. If the copyright was registered, the copyright owner may be entitled to statutory damages. These are the amounts set by law for various infringement categories, regardless of the actual costs. For instance, the court can award an amount between $200 and $150,000, depending on whether the infringement was innocent or willful.[3]

THE FOUR FACTORS FOR DETERMINING FAIR USE

From a legal standpoint, determining fair use can be complicated. The law is based on four factors, which balance a copyright owner's rights with other people's right to fair use.

The first factor concerns the purpose of the intended use, including whether it is for commercial or nonprofit use. In *Warner Brothers Entertainment, Inc. v. RDR Books*, for example, RDR Books clearly intended to make a profit from the Harry Potter reference guide. The question was whether the guide transformed the original work enough to create something new. While the nature of the guide (an encyclopedia) was

PERMISSIONS

People must seek permission when they wish to use copyrighted material beyond the scope of fair use. For example, an author may wish to include a copyrighted poem in a novel. Obtaining permission from the copyright holder would avoid unlawful use of the work. The author must first identify the copyright owner. It may or may not be the poet, as copyright can be transferred. The copyright owner has the right to refuse permission. If granting permission, the owner also has a right to charge a fee.

Fair use is limited for fiction, such as the Harry Potter series, because of its unique, imaginative nature.

substantially different from the original works (novels), the court ruled that the guide relied too heavily on the copyrighted works to be considered fair use.

The second factor is the nature of the original copyrighted work. Fair use is allowed less for fictional works, such as the Harry Potter series, than for factual works. That is because a fictional work typically reflects the unique thoughts of the author, whereas a reference book typically reflects the thoughts of many authors and researchers in the field.

THE DA VINCI CODE

Published in 2003, *The Da Vinci Code* by Dan Brown became one of the most successful novels of all time. It dominated best-seller lists, and it sold more than 40 million copies by April 2006.[4] That May, a movie based on the book was scheduled for release. But then media attention shifted to a trial in London, England, where Brown was accused of stealing copyrighted ideas for the book.

Brown's controversial novel included many of the same ideas and theories as *The Holy Blood and the Holy Grail*, a nonfiction book published in 1982. Authors Michael Baigent and Richard Leigh sued Brown's publisher for copyright infringement. They claimed Brown had copied a substantial number of their ideas and the sequence of facts from their work.

Lawyers for Random House, Brown's publisher, argued that *The Holy Blood and the Holy Grail* was just one of many sources Brown consulted and that he referenced the book in his novel. The basic ideas in both books were not original and were based on historical theories in many sources.

Judge Peter Smith, applying British copyright law nearly identical to American law, ruled that Brown was not guilty of

copyright infringement. The judgment indicated Brown had used *The Holy Blood and the Holy Grail*, along with other sources, as general background material for writing *The Da Vinci Code*. That is, he had copied facts and ideas—which are not protected by copyright—from Baigent and Leigh's work, but he did not infringe on their unique expression.

The third factor is the amount of the copyrighted work that is used. It is not based solely on a word count but rather on an analysis of how important the copied material is to the original work. Guidelines consider both quantity (how much) and quality (how important). For example, the court found that the *Harry Potter Lexicon* used more of the original books than was reasonably necessary. In effect, Vander Ark copied 450 pages of materials from the Harry Potter series.[5]

The fourth factor determines whether the new work interferes with the original work's marketability, or the ability for the copyright owner to earn money from the original work. The court ruled the *Harry Potter Lexicon* could harm sales of Rowling's two companion books to the series. In addition, the guide could harm the potential market for her own encyclopedia or other derivative works.

FAIR OR NOT FAIR?

Applying the four factors for fair use can result in different legal decisions in similar cases. In 1988, artist Faith Ringgold granted a museum the right to produce a poster depicting her art piece *Church Picnic*. In 1997, Ringgold sued Black Entertainment Television (BET) for featuring the poster several times on a sitcom series. Most artwork—as well as logos and products—featured on television and in movies is either

> **"** Fair use is one of the most unsettled areas of the law. The doctrine has been said to be so flexible as to virtually defy definition. **"** [6]
>
> —Judge David A. Nelson, *Princeton University Press v. Michigan Document Services* (1996)

A court ruled that the BET network had infringed upon artist Faith Ringgold's copyright.

licensed for a fee or used with permission. But BET used the *Church Picnic* poster without any authorization.

The court ruled that BET's use of the poster was infringement. The image had not been transformed, and the poster was used in the same way as the original—as decorative art. The unauthorized display of the poster on television could impact the owner's ability to license the work for similar purposes.

In a similar case, Joe Baraban owned the rights to a photograph he licensed in 1993 for an advertisement supporting nuclear energy. Then, in 1997, author Gerald Celente and publisher Time Warner used a small black-and-white reproduction of the advertisement in a book that criticized the nuclear energy industry. Baraban sued for infringement in 2000.

In this situation, the court ruled that the reproduced image was considered fair use. The image had been used for the purpose of criticism. The photograph had been cropped, and the small image would not likely impact the market for the original photo or advertisement.

Copyright infringement can be costly, even if it was not done purposely. Many creators avoid copyright infringement issues by using works in the public domain, which are not protected by copyright.

Fair use must be determined on a case-by-case basis in copyright lawsuits.

CHAPTER 4

PUBLIC DOMAIN

In 2011, British photographer David Slater visited a nature reserve on the Indonesian island of Sulawesi to take pictures of rare macaque monkeys. When he left his camera unattended, the curious monkeys grabbed it. The result was a series of hilarious self-portraits. Naruto the monkey took a particularly charming selfie with a huge grin. The snap made him one of the most famous monkeys in the world—but it also made him the focus of a copyright lawsuit in 2015. The case would raise many questions about copyright protection and the public domain.

Slater published a book containing the monkey photos and sold it in the United States. Then People for the Ethical Treatment of Animals (PETA), an animal rights organization, sued Slater and the publishing company on behalf of Naruto. PETA claimed the monkey was the creator of the photograph and therefore owned the copyright.

PETA's lawsuit raised the question of whether a monkey can own a copyright. Legal analysts said the answer likely is no. To be protected by copyright under US copyright law, a work must have an author, and an author is specifically defined as a human. As a

Naruto's selfie became an important case in US copyright history.

result of this case, the US Copyright Office clarified it would not register works created by animals, plants, or nature.

The lawsuit also raised the question of whether Slater could claim copyright ownership of the monkey selfie. Legal analysts again said this is unlikely. Since the photographer did not create the work or own the monkey, he was not entitled to copyright protection. And seeing as neither the monkey nor Slater could claim copyright, the photograph was in the public domain. Anyone could use it without permission.

> ❝ Imagining a monkey as the copyright 'author' in Title 17 of the United States Code is a farcical journey Dr. Seuss might have written. ❞ [1]
>
> —Andrew J. Dhuey, David Slater's attorney

WHAT IS THE PUBLIC DOMAIN?

Creative works that are not protected by copyright are in the public domain. Works in the public domain are available for anyone to use in any way they wish. Creators of public domain works control no exclusive rights, and no one else can obtain the copyright protection. Once something is in the public domain, it usually remains there forever.

Both copyright protection and the public domain encourage creativity, though in different ways. Copyright allows creators to earn money from new works they create. In contrast, the public domain provides a pool of creative works others may draw on to create new works. Using public domain works is very cost-effective. Obtaining permission for a copyrighted work can cost thousands of dollars. But public domain works are typically free. In some cases,

When a work enters the public domain, it usually remains there—but not always. In 1994, Congress passed a law that restored US copyright protection to certain foreign works that had been in the public domain for years.

Conductor Lawrence Golan and his University of Denver orchestras performed many public domain pieces, such as the works of Russian composer Igor Stravinsky. Those pieces were quite inexpensive compared with copyrighted pieces. Then suddenly these foreign works were no longer available, once their copyrights were restored.

Golan and other groups, including the Fair Use Project, challenged the law. They felt that restoring copyright protection was unconstitutional and that it undermined the purpose and integrity of the public domain. But ultimately, in *Golan v. Holder* (2012), the Supreme Court upheld the congressional law that restored the copyrights.

there may be a small fee to access some public domain materials in private archives or government collections.

Billions of works are in the public domain. These include classic literature, art, and music as well as some newly published works. Works enter the public domain for a variety of reasons. Many were published or created before there was a copyright law. In other cases, copyright was never acquired, or the works were never entitled to copyright in the first place. Some material's copyright was lost or has expired. And some creators donated their works to the public domain.

USING WORK IN THE PUBLIC DOMAIN

Individuals are free to use public domain works. There is no infringement and no penalties. Web developers can use public domain photos to enhance their websites. Librarians can make

Dozens of Disney movies, including *Aladdin*, are based on public domain material.

copies of public domain works for their collections. Theater groups can adapt and perform public domain plays. And authors can create new stories using characters from public domain works.

Many popular works are actually adaptations of public domain material. In particular, this includes many famous movies. For example, the musical *Les Misérables* is based on a public domain novel by Victor Hugo. At least 50 Disney films, including *Aladdin* and *Alice in Wonderland*, are based on public domain stories.[2] *The Secret Garden*, a children's classic written by Frances Hodgson Burnett, has been made into a TV movie, a musical, a film, a cookbook, an ebook, a video, and two audiobooks.

ORPHAN WORKS

Orphan works fall somewhere between copyright protection and the public domain. When a work's creator or copyright owner cannot be identified or located, the creation is considered an orphan work. These works are granted copyright protection—even though no one claims them.

> "The persistent problem of orphan works is due mostly to three dangerous and sadly persistent aspects of U. S. copyright law: extremely long terms, high statutory damages, and a lack of formalities for copyright protection."[3]
>
> —Corynne McSherry of the Electronic Frontier Foundation

Supporters of the public domain argue that orphan works should not be protected. They point out that orphaned works are harmed, not helped, by copyright protection. For example, an orphan movie on filmstrip cannot be preserved into a digital form. That is an exclusive right protected by its copyright. But with no copyright owner to take action and no access for others to even seek permission, the filmstrip may ultimately deteriorate, and the movie may be lost forever. In the same fashion, digital libraries cannot acquire and preserve orphan works. Writers, artists, and musicians cannot transform the orphan works into new material.

PUBLIC DOMAIN OR COPYRIGHTED?

Determining whether a work is in the public domain is not always easy. Incorrectly assuming a work is available in the public domain may lead to copyright infringement.

For safest use of online materials, several websites provide lists of public domain works. Project Gutenberg, the oldest digital library, offers thousands of works in the public domain in the United States, though some may be protected in other countries. The Library of Congress also has a large digital collection of public domain documents. Cornell University maintains a helpful chart summarizing copyright protection terms. In complicated cases, however, individuals may require the help of attorneys.

Even the US Copyright Office states, "Orphan works are a frustration, a liability risk, and a major cause of gridlock in the digital marketplace."[4] Many people balk at using orphan works because they are afraid the copyright owners might suddenly surface and sue them. Reform may be on the horizon. Many proposals have been made to resolve the issues of orphan works.

PUBLIC DOMAIN AND COPYRIGHT DURATION

Each year on January 1, the Center for the Study of the Public Domain celebrates Public Domain Day—the date when a new batch of copyrights expire and works pass into the public domain. Since the late 1990s, though, there has been nothing to celebrate, as no works published in the United States have passed into the public domain.

Critics argue that orphan works such as old films are at risk of being lost forever.

SONNY BONO COPYRIGHT TERM EXTENSION ACT (1998)

Because of earlier revisions to US copyright law, protection for works published in the 1920s was scheduled to expire in the 1990s. So in 1998, President Bill Clinton signed into law the Sonny Bono Copyright Term Extension Act. The law was named in honor of Representative Sonny Bono, a former songwriter and performer. The law extended the terms of almost all existing copyrights for 20 years. As 2018 approaches, lawmakers may again debate whether to enact a new extension or allow older works to fall under current terms and enter the public domain.

Many copyright holders and other supporters applauded the new law. But electronic publisher Eric Eldred was a chief opponent. He believed it limited public access for creators who wished to legally use older works. Many opponents referred to the law as the "Mickey Mouse Protection Act." The term partly referred to how the Walt Disney Corporation heavily lobbied for the bill to extend copyright protection for its mascot. But the term also reflected how opponents felt the law was "Mickey Mouse," or not to be taken seriously.

Eldred and his supporters argued that the Bono Act was unconstitutional. But in *Eldred v. Ashcroft* (2003), the Supreme Court upheld the copyright term extensions.

This is due to the Sonny Bono Copyright Term Extension Act of 1998, which extended nearly all copyright terms by 20 years.

Some people applaud extension of copyright duration. Others do not. On one hand, those supporting artists' rights argue in favor of the economic benefits. They claim that extensions give copyright holders more years to earn income from their works. On the other hand, opponents argue that extensions generally do not financially benefit copyright owners enough to justify keeping the public from using those older works in new ways. A Congressional

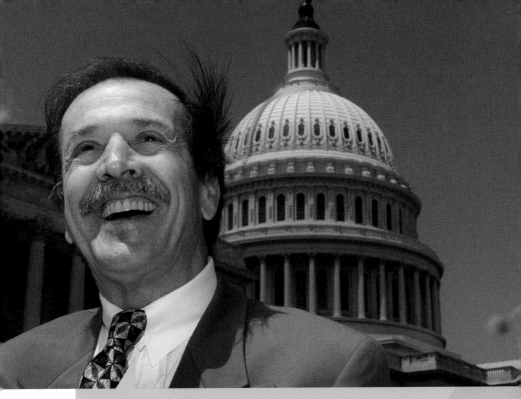

Representative Sonny Bono was the namesake of a controversial bill extending copyright protection for many works.

Research Service study revealed that only 2 percent of works retain commercial value when they are between 55 and 75 years old.[5]

> "There's no evidence suggesting that a longer term is going to produce any more art, literature. The only reason to extend the term is to give private benefits to companies like Disney or Time Warner that have valuable properties like Mickey Mouse or famous films."[6]
>
> —Chris Sprigman, legal scholar

Copyright extension is not the only issue creating debate. Another hotly debated issue is whether creative works should be viewed as property, similar to possessions. The topic of intellectual property explores this idea.

CHAPTER 5

INTELLECTUAL PROPERTY

The term *intellectual property* refers to "creations of the mind."[1] Inventions, literary works, films, music, art, designs, symbols, slogans, logos, and more are all considered intellectual property. Even though intellectual property covers a wide range of creations, each category is unique. Therefore, different laws protect the different kinds of intellectual property, even if they have several similarities.

In particular, separate laws protect copyrights, patents, and trademarks, but they all stem from Article I, Section 8 of the US Constitution. Patent laws and copyright laws are based on Clause 8, which gives Congress the power to grant authors and inventors protection for their works for a limited time. Trademark laws, on the other hand, are based on Clause 3. That clause grants Congress the power to regulate trade. Trademark protection can last forever because it is not limited by term, as are copyrights and patents. However, trademark registration must be renewed according to federal or state laws.

Many types of ideas, creations, and concepts fall within the category of intellectual property.

PATENT PENDING

The time between applying for and obtaining a patent can be years. In the meantime, an inventor may sell products marked "patent pending." This phrase indicates that the inventor has applied to the USPTO for patent protection. It does not guarantee that a patent will be obtained.

While a patent is pending, an inventor cannot sue another person for making, using, or selling the invention. The patent pending mark has no legal effect, but it may discourage others from copying the invention.

As copyright laws protect the artists behind creative works, patent laws protect the inventors behind innovative devices and processes. Patent laws grant inventors the right to exclude others from making, using, selling, or importing their works. Patents protect any new and beneficial process, machine, article of manufacture, or improvement.

Successfully obtaining a patent is a complex and lengthy process that usually requires the legal expertise of a patent attorney. When applying for a patent, the inventor must research whether another inventor has already made the same invention public or offered it for sale. The application and processing fees can cost thousands of dollars, and it can take years to finally receive a patent. The US Patent and Trademark Office (USPTO) receives hundreds of thousands of patent applications a year, and only roughly half of them are granted.

COMPARING PATENTS AND COPYRIGHTS

Because patents and copyrights share the same constitutional source, they are alike in some ways. Both protect works rather than ideas. Both limit the duration of protection. Both provide for legal action against infringement.

But in other ways, patents and copyrights are very different. Copyright protection begins as soon as a creator puts a work in permanent form. Patent protection is not only costly but much more difficult to obtain. And whereas the length of copyright protection varies, based on when a work was created, patent protection generally lasts 14 or 20 years from the date of application.

TRADEMARKS

A trademark is a sign, symbol, word, or phrase that represents an individual or a company. The Nike swoosh, McDonald's golden arches, and the NBC network's peacock are examples. Unlike copyrights and patents, trademarks do not encourage the growth of human knowledge. Instead, trademarks help buyers easily recognize the source of a product or service. When consumers see a swoosh on

TRADEMARK SYMBOLS

There is no legal requirement to use a trademark symbol, but it is recommended as a way to discourage infringement. The symbol ™ is used for products, and ℠ is used for services. These symbols are used for unregistered trademarks. A federal registration symbol, expressed as ®, may be used only if the trademark is registered. Registering a trademark is not required, but it provides advantages in court proceedings, similar to registering a copyright.

The Nike swoosh is one of the most recognizable trademarks in the world.

a pair of shoes, for example, they immediately know the shoes are a Nike product. Trademark law is based on the commerce clause of the Constitution because it helps prevent confusion in the marketplace.

A trademark is protected as soon as it is used on goods or services for customers. The longer a trademark is used, the

stronger it becomes because it builds recognition. A trademark does not have to be registered to be protected by law. However, registering a trademark under federal and state laws helps prevent other businesses from using the same words, signs, or symbols to identify their products.

> "Everyone has the right to the protection of the moral and material interests resulting from any scientific, literary, or artistic production of which he is the author." [2]
>
> —United Nations, *Universal Declaration of Human Rights*

INTELLECTUAL PROPERTY RIGHTS

Another form of intellectual property is the right of publicity or persona. This is a person's right to control the use of his or her name, likeness, and persona to sell products and services. It is an intellectual property right typically governed by state law. Laws protecting the right of publicity are similar in some ways to those protecting trademarks. A name and likeness are a kind of personal brand. Laws prevent unauthorized use of anyone's personal brand to sell products. The right of publicity is most often associated with celebrities, whose names or images may generate sales.

In 2009, Dominick's Finer Foods grocery chain used the name and identity of basketball legend Michael Jordan without permission. Dominick's full-page advertisement gave the impression that Jordan endorsed a brand of steak the store was selling.

Basketball legend Michael Jordan protected his right to publicity in a lawsuit.

Jordan sued the grocery chain, stating that he would never permit Dominick's to use his identity. Among many other business interests, Jordan was associated with two steak restaurants that bore his name. Jordan claimed this unauthorized use of publicity to sell Dominick's steaks was especially damaging, as it conflicted with his own restaurants. The court awarded Jordan a settlement of $8.9 million, which he later donated to charity.³

INTELLECTUAL PROPERTY DEBATE

Some people object to using *intellectual property* as an umbrella term for many different kinds of issues. They point out that literary works, inventions, trademarks, and personal identities are very different and require separate kinds of protection. Critics believe generalizing them all under the intellectual property label leads to confusion.

Other people object to using the word *property* to refer to works of the mind. They point out that *property* generally refers to physical objects, such as land, buildings, or possessions. But critics stress that artistic creations, trademarks, and personas are not physical, tangible items. Some critics object to concepts such as copyright "theft" or "piracy" because they take the property analogy too far.⁴

Despite debates over terminology, it is important to understand the different kinds of intellectual property and the laws that protect them. This is true for people who use the works as well as for those who create them.

CHAPTER 6

COPYRIGHTS AND SCHOOLS

Copyright is important to authors, artists, and other creators. But it is also important to students and teachers. In school settings, students create new works protected by copyright, and teachers and students use existing copyrighted works in class. A balance must be made: schools need access to copyrighted material to advance knowledge and learning, and copyright owners need to protect their work and interests.

Turnitin is a company that uses technology to detect plagiarism in student papers. Thousands of high schools and colleges across the United States use the company's services. When they electronically submit papers to Turnitin, students must enter a clickwrap agreement that grants the company permission to archive, or store, their papers in a database. That is, by clicking the "I agree" box on Turnitin's website, students grant the company permission to archive, or store, their papers in a database.

In 2008, four US high school students sued Turnitin. The students claimed that Turnitin's archiving their work was a copyright violation. Part of the students' argument indicated

When students create new works in school, copyright protection immediately applies.

Plagiarism checkers such as Turnitin help identify material that has been copied from other sources. The software compares the text of a submitted paper with texts in a database. Databases may consist of Internet content, other students' archived papers, journal articles, books, and research manuscripts.

A plagiarism checker provides a report to the teacher indicating the percentage of material that came from other sources. However, a match does not automatically mean the submitted text was plagiarized. Only a human can decide that. For instance, the matched text may be a properly used and credited quote within fair use guidelines.

The purpose of plagiarism checkers is to discourage cheating, but some people say they are not effective. A study of some college students in California showed that students continued to plagiarize even though they knew their work would be analyzed by a plagiarism checker.

their concern about their rights to submit their papers elsewhere. For example, if they used the same papers for college admission applications and the colleges used Turnitin, the students might be accused of plagiarism because the same papers existed in the database.

In *A.V. v. iParadigms, L.L.C.* (2009), the court decided in favor of Turnitin. The court applied the four factors of fair use. First, Turnitin's use of the student papers was highly transformative and not derivative. It did not build on the works but merely checked them for plagiarism. Second, Turnitin's use did not discourage students' creativity in any way. Third, while Turnitin did use the entire text of the papers, doing so was necessary to complete a thorough plagiarism check. And fourth, Turnitin did not harm but rather protected the future marketability of students' works

By following the fair use guidelines, students can include copyrighted material in projects and presentations.

by preventing others from using the works. The case proved that although students' work is protected by copyright, it—like all copyrighted material—is limited to some degree by fair use.

FAIR USE GUIDELINES FOR STUDENTS

Understanding copyright is critical for students because they not only create their own material but also use others' materials. For instance, students often quote or paraphrase material from copyrighted works in their papers. They also use copyrighted or trademarked images, music, or multimedia in classroom presentations.

Fair use often covers the use of copyrighted or trademarked works for classroom assignments or projects. For instance, a student's using a small part of a copyrighted work—only what is needed for the purpose of the project—would likely be considered fair use under the four factors. In particular, the fourth factor of market effect depends on the amount of time the project is available and the number of people with access to it. If a student uses copyrighted material in a project for a small group, such as a single class, the use is more likely to be considered fair than if the student posted the project online.

In situations where fair use is questionable, many students seek permission to use copyrighted or trademarked materials. Students may also choose to use works in the public domain, avoiding copyright issues entirely. It is important, however, for students to cite sources in order to avoid plagiarism—whether working with copyrighted materials or those in the public domain.

FAIR USE GUIDELINES FOR TEACHERS

Like students, teachers may also wish to use copyrighted material in a school setting. Examples include copies of stories, poems, or pictures to teach a particular skill or lesson. Teachers might also need charts, graphs, or diagrams to help students understand a concept. Copyright law allows teachers special considerations for fair use, but use is still limited.

> **"** Teachers are in an incongruent position of trying to push the limits of the fair use exception at the same time that they have an obligation to teach students about respect for copyright law. **"** [1]
>
> —Nancy Willard,
> copyright attorney

Prior to the Copyright Act of 1976, some schools incorrectly interpreted the fair use law. Specifically, they misunderstood the first factor, which considers whether material is used for commercial or nonprofit educational purposes. Some teachers assumed they could use any copyrighted material in any way, so long as it was educational and they did not make a profit. This was not true.

The Copyright Act of 1976 helped establish some minimal guidelines for schools. For instance, the 1976 guidelines specified that making multiple copies of copyrighted material for a classroom is considered fair use under certain circumstances. The copying must meet the requirements of brevity, spontaneity, and cumulative effect.

Brevity refers to the amount of a copyrighted work that can be copied under fair use. Teachers must follow specific numbers.

Before sharing copyrighted material in the classroom, teachers must meet the fair use factors.

For example, fair use allows teachers to use a complete work of fewer than 2,500 words or a poem of fewer than 250 words. For a longer work, fair use allows an excerpt of fewer than 1,000 words or 10 percent of a text, whichever is less.

The spontaneity factor allows copying under unanticipated circumstances when teachers do not have time to request permission. For example, a teacher might discover an article in a magazine that would be useful for the next day's lesson. The time between the teacher's decision to copy the material and the actual use of the copies in the classroom must be short. In contrast, if teachers know at least three weeks in advance that they want to reproduce copyrighted material, they must request permission.

Finally, the cumulative effect factor dictates that copied material must be used for only one course term. Copying also cannot be a substitute for buying a copyrighted work or getting enough copies of the work for the class. Workbooks and standardized tests may never be copied.

Similar guidelines apply to the fair use of copyrighted music in school. Music teachers can copy excerpts of sheet music as long as they do not exceed 10 percent of the work. Only one copy per student is permitted. The guidelines for musical performances depend on whether the performance is public. If no performance fees are charged, or if fees go to charitable causes, school bands or orchestras may perform copyrighted music under fair use. But a school band playing at a fee-based event, such as a football game, is considered a public performance.

SHOWING RECORDED PROGRAMS IN SCHOOLS

In addition to using copyrighted text and music, teachers and school librarians may wish to show copyrighted television programs and movies as teaching aids. Under the fair use guidelines, teachers can record television programs from network or cable stations and show them in the classroom. A teacher may show the program only once within ten days of recording. The recording must then be erased or destroyed after 45 days.

The right to use copyrighted works is not the same in distance education as in traditional classrooms. Distance education allows students to learn from locations other than schools and traditional classroom settings. Many distance education programs feature online learning.

The TEACH Act of 2002 provides copyright exceptions for distance education. Teachers may prepare course websites that include copyrighted works for the purpose of teaching. The materials may be available for a short time—usually as long as needed for distance students to meet the requirements of the lesson.

That said, some teachers consider the responsibilities and limits of the TEACH Act confusing and difficult to follow. In order to avoid infringement claims, they prefer to rely on permission or fair use of materials for distance education.

The Copyright Act of 1976 allows teachers or librarians to show legally obtained movies or videos in classrooms or in other face-to-face teaching situations. Fair use does not extend to entertainment settings, however, such as an after-school movie night for students and families. Streaming films to students' homes or other remote locations is also not permitted by this exception.

From the perspective of both students and teachers, schools serve as unique backdrops for fair use guidelines and copyright laws. The rise of the Internet and digital technology also created— and continues to create—unique situations for copyright.

Copyright rules for school bands depend on whether the performance is fee based.

CHAPTER 7

COPYRIGHTS IN THE DIGITAL AGE

In 2004, the search engine Google announced plans to create a digital library. Teaming with major publishers and libraries, the company would scan millions of printed books from libraries around the United States. Google's purpose was to provide users with a searchable collection of online books. Many of those books were protected by copyright, but Google did not seek permission or compensate copyright holders. In 2005, the project became known as Google Books.

That same year, the Authors Guild, an organization of published authors, sued Google for copyright infringement. In *Authors Guild v. Google*, the authors claimed the digital library had a damaging effect on authors' potential income. Readers could access portions of the works for free, which they argued could reduce sales opportunities. Using intellectual property terms, the organization viewed "Google's seizure of property as a serious threat to writers and their livelihoods."[1]

Ten years of lawsuits and trials came to a conclusion in 2015. A US court of appeals upheld a 2013 district court's decision

By featuring snippets from millions of copyrighted books, Google Books became part of a landmark court battle.

in favor of Google. A judge ruled that Google Books was a fair use of copyrighted works. The searchable function was a highly transformative use of the books. The snippets, or small portions of text, were within fair use guidelines. And because users could not read entire works, Google Books did not impact the market for authors' copyrighted books.

> **❝** While authors are undoubtedly important intended beneficiaries of copyright, the ultimate, primary intended beneficiary is the public. **❞** [2]
>
> —Judge Pierre Leval, *Authors Guild v. Google*

Despite the district court's ruling, the Authors Guild remained committed to seeking compensation for the use of copyrighted works. In the meantime, Google's victory helped clarify fair use in the digital age and perhaps provided incentive for broader digital access to works.

COPYRIGHTS AND INTERNET MATERIAL

Some people incorrectly believe everything on the Internet is in the public domain. But just because online material can be easily copied, cut and pasted, or downloaded does not mean it is not copyrighted. Work first created online—whether art, literature, or a simple personal blog—is automatically protected by copyright, as it is placed in permanent form. And when previously existing work is posted on the Internet, it is still protected by copyright. For instance, a book originally printed on paper does not lose its copyright protection when it becomes an ebook.

A printed book and its ebook version are covered by the same original copyright.

Actually, it is safe to assume that everything on the Internet is copyrighted unless it is clearly marked as public domain from a trusted source. This means individuals must seek permission to use copyrighted material on the Internet or follow fair use guidelines.

DIGITAL MILLENNIUM COPYRIGHT ACT

The digital age posed a challenge to existing copyright laws, especially as new technology seemed to appear overnight. To help address this, the Digital Millennium Copyright Act (DMCA) went into effect in 2000.

The law is divided into sections that address copyright issues in the digital age. For example, it provides rules that protect electronic access to copyrighted works. The DMCA was Congress's first attempt to move US copyright law into the digital age. Congress considers it part of an ongoing process to keep US copyright law current with changing technology. According to the Executive Summary of the DMCA, Congress realized "the only thing that remains constant is change."[3]

SAFE HARBOR

One aspect of the DMCA is the safe harbor provision for Internet service providers (ISPs). An ISP is a company that provides Internet access, web hosting, and other online services. Technically, ISPs are responsible for all material posted on their websites, including material that infringes on

> "Through enactment of the Digital Millennium Copyright Act, we have done our best to protect from digital piracy the copyright industries that comprise the leading export of the United States."[4]
>
> —President Bill Clinton on signing the DMCA

copyright. They are also responsible for cached material, which is stored information. But the DMCA recognizes how difficult it would be for an ISP to screen every post or site by every user.

For this reason, the safe harbor provision protects ISPs when their users violate copyright law. When ISPs comply with safe harbor requirements, they cannot be held liable for copyright infringement that was not their fault. By removing responsibility for infringement, this protection for service providers eventually resulted in Internet sites such as YouTube.

To qualify for safe harbor protection, an ISP must ensure that copyright owners can easily identify the owner of a website. In cases of infringement, an ISP must comply with an order to take down copyrighted material from a website and notify the person who posted it.

DMCA TAKEDOWN NOTICE

Under the DMCA, a copyright owner—or someone authorized to act on behalf of the owner—can request that a website owner remove infringed material from a website. The request is called a takedown notice. The takedown notice must include certain information. It must identify the infringed material and confirm that permission was not given. After receiving a takedown notice, a person or ISP must remove the infringed material or block access to it. Infringement may also result in a substantial penalty.

Before a copyright owner issues a takedown notice, fair use must be taken into account. Upon receiving a notice, the person who posted the material has an opportunity to defend against the accusation. If a court determines the copyrighted material is fair use, the copyright owner may be penalized for the unwarranted takedown notice.

DIGITAL REPRODUCTIONS

The DMCA makes it especially important for Internet users and website owners to understand copyright laws and fair use guidelines. One area of note is digital reproductions of existing works. Digitizing a work does not create a new work. The original copyright still applies.

For example, using a digitized copyrighted image without permission is infringement. In particular, the sharing mechanisms on social networking sites may raise legal issues. For example, Pinterest encourages users to post anything they find interesting.

Pinterest is a helpful place to post interesting online material, but few users consider the copyright ramifications.

If the material is copyrighted, however, users may violate copyright law if they post it without permission.

Fair use of copyrighted digital images is permitted under certain circumstances, such as for research, news reporting, or criticism. The four factors of fair use apply. For instance, transforming an image by incorporating it into an educational video would likely be fair use. Using a thumbnail or a portion is

MUSIC STREAMING

In the past, music lovers needed to purchase hard media, such as a compact disc, or a digital copy in order to listen to their favorite songs. Today, many listeners access music through digital music-streaming services such as Pandora and Google Play. For a fee, subscribers can listen to music via a streaming service without purchasing copies of the music. The top music-streaming services boast music libraries of at least 20 million songs.[5]

Music streaming is quite popular. But it is also the focus of ongoing debate. Online music-streaming service providers follow copyright laws. Through special provisions in the Copyright Act, they pay royalties to record companies, songwriters, and musicians. For this reason, some copyright owners in the music industry support online streaming as a way to create income. But other copyright owners argue that the shift from album sales to digital streaming has negatively impacted their income.

more likely to be considered fair use than using an exact copy of the entire image. Whether a use impacts the marketability of the image is typically decided on a case-by-case basis.

DIGITAL SOUND RECORDINGS

Today, most sound recordings are captured as digital signals. The recordings can be played on computers and other digital technology. Before the digital age, most songs, albums, and other audio works were recorded as analog signals, which are not computerized. When technology advanced, musicians and companies converted the analog recordings to digital signals. A digital copy of an analog sound recording is considered a derivative work.

Given this protection, people such as Joel Tenenbaum were guilty of copyright infringement after illegally downloading and distributing digital music from file-sharing sites. Each of those digital songs were protected by the original recording's copyright. In *A&M Records, Inc. v. Napster, Inc.* (2001), unauthorized downloading or sharing of music files was ruled illegal.

Even more changes to copyright laws may be needed as technology evolves. New technology complicates copyright law for creators, users, and lawmakers alike. Another complication is the fact that copyright law varies from country to country. International copyright is a complex matter in and of itself.

COPYRIGHT PROTECTION FOR SOUND RECORDINGS

Federal law provides copyright protection for sound recordings produced on or after February 15, 1972. Copyright protection for sound recordings created before that date is up to the laws of individual states. That covers everything recorded between the mid–1800s to the hits of performers such as Elvis Presley and the Beatles in the early 1970s.

The duration of protection varies from state to state, but most recordings will not enter the public domain until 2067. Services such as Sirius XM and Pandora have been sued for streaming pre–1972 recordings without permission or payment of fees. The Copyright Office has recommended that Congress make all sound recordings subject to the same protection under federal copyright law.

NAPSTER AND THE DIGITAL MUSIC REVOLUTION

In the 1990s, before software such as iTunes, downloading music via the Internet was an unreliable and time-consuming process. Then 17-year-old Shawn Fanning invented software that revolutionized the way people accessed music.

Fanning, with the help of Sean Parker, launched Napster in 1999. Napster was a peer-to-peer file-sharing service that allowed people access to MP3s, a type of digital music file, on each other's computers. Users could share and download the music without cost. Users especially appreciated being able to download single songs, rather than entire albums. An article in *Time* magazine in 2000 said Napster "ranks among the greatest Internet applications ever."[6]

By March 2000, Napster had 20 million users. A year later, it had 57 million users.[7] Most users had little or no understanding of the legal issues involved in downloading copyrighted music.

The Record Industry Association of America (RIAA) and many musicians sued Napster and its users for copyright infringement.

Millions of users shared copyrighted music files on Napster before a court decision forced the service to shut down.

The lawsuit caused heated debate. Napster argued it did not store any MP3 files on its servers; it merely enabled users to share their music with each other. Musicians were divided on the issue. Some enjoyed the attention their songs received. Others criticized Fanning and Parker as outright thieves, stealing music without paying for it.

Ultimately, Napster was found guilty of copyright infringement in *A&M Records v. Napster* (2001). Unauthorized downloading of music files was ruled illegal, and the service was forced to shut down.

CHAPTER 8

GLOBAL COPYRIGHT ISSUES

Supap Kirtsaeng came to the United States from Thailand in 1997 as a college student. He discovered that textbooks were available at much lower prices in Thailand. Kirtsaeng asked friends back in Thailand to buy textbooks and ship them to him. He then resold the books on eBay at a profit. John Wiley and Sons, an American publishing company, printed some of the textbooks Kirtsaeng imported and sold. In 2008, Wiley sued Kirtsaeng for copyright infringement. They argued that they alone had such rights to sales.

Wiley's case was based on a part of US copyright law that prohibits importing copies of works without permission. In turn, Kirtsaeng's defense was based on another part of US copyright law known as the first sale doctrine. For instance, the copyright owner controls the first sale of a book, but the person who buys the book can then resell it without permission.

Supap Kirtsaeng came under legal fire when he sold imported copies of textbooks.

A district court ruled against Kirtsaeng, and a court of appeals agreed with the decision. The case eventually went to the Supreme Court. The question was whether a copy legally acquired abroad and then imported into the United States could be resold without permission. Many people eagerly awaited the decision. If the court ruled in Wiley's favor, museums, libraries, and used-book sellers would have to obtain licensing rights for works they imported and distributed.

In *Kirtsaeng v. John Wiley & Sons, Inc.* (2013), the Supreme Court reversed the lower courts' decision. The ruling stated that the first sale doctrine did not have geographic restrictions. Someone who legally owns a copy of a copyrighted work has the right to resell the work without permission, regardless of where the work was manufactured. The case was an interesting example of copyright law complexities inside—and especially outside—US borders.

> " The concept of reselling foreign records or books has been around for decades. But the Internet—eBay in the case of Kirtsaeng—has now made this a major issue for publishers. "[1]
>
> —Glenn Pudelka, copyright attorney

INTERNATIONAL COPYRIGHT LAWS

There is no universal copyright law that protects a work throughout the world. Copyright protection depends on the individual laws of each country. However, many countries extend protection to foreign works under certain conditions. International treaties and conventions set these conditions. There

COPYRIGHT CHANGES IN THE UNITED KINGDOM

In the United Kingdom, the Copyright, Designs and Patents Act 1988 protected the rights of the creators of written, musical, and visual works. Although the law included some fair use exceptions, it did not provide for people with disabilities. For instance, it did not allow someone with a visual impairment to create an accessible copy of a copyrighted work without seeking permission. Accessible copies for people who are blind or visually impaired include braille, audio, e-text, or other formats.

In 2003, the Copyright (Visually Impaired Persons) Act 2002 came into effect in the United Kingdom. This law made it possible for people who are visually impaired to make accessible copies without seeking copyright owners' permission.

Then, in 2014, copyright law was reformed to benefit people with impairments that prevented or restricted them from accessing creative content. It permitted educational establishments—including colleges and universities, nonprofit organizations, and charities—to make copyrighted materials more accessible to learners with disabilities. Betty Willder, a legal information specialist, said, "These changes are a positive step forward in bringing copyright law up-to-date with the digital learning environment and accessibility needs."[2]

are international agreements that protect patents and trademarks as well.

It can be difficult to navigate the differences in copyright laws from nation to nation. For example, US copyright laws protect creators' economic rights—the rights to control their works and to profit from them. In many other countries, though, copyright laws protect creators' moral rights. These include the right to be identified as the creator of a work, the right to prevent alteration or destruction of a work, and the right to decide when to release a work to the public. Moral rights cannot always be transferred to

another person, and they may last forever. This may dramatically limit others' ability to use a work created in a country protecting moral, rather than economic, rights.

Duration of copyright protection also varies from country to country. Some countries granted copyright extensions to works published during World War I (1914–1918) or World War II (1939–1945) or to works whose creators participated in or died during a war. Due to such differences, some works do not enter the public domain at the same time in all countries. A collection of national copyright laws is available through the United Nations Educational, Scientific and Cultural Organization.

BERNE CONVENTION

The Berne Convention is an international organization that establishes minimum international standards of protection. The standards involve the types of works protected, duration of protection, and limitations to protection. As of 2014, the organization had 168 member nations, including the United States.[3] Members of the Berne Convention agree to grant the same copyright protection to creative works produced in other countries as to works produced

> By ratifying Berne, the United States announced its choice to advance the progress of literature and the arts internationally by providing substantial copyright protection to authors and artists of all nations.[4]
>
> —Senator Orrin Hatch, 1989

In a global market, copyright law protects creative works in different ways in different countries.

in their own country. No formalities, such as copyright notice or registration, are required.

The Berne Convention does not offer universal protection. Works not covered under the Berne Convention may still receive copyright protection under a foreign country's laws or by a treaty between that country and the country of origin. However, a few countries offer little or no copyright protection to any foreign works. And some countries do not maintain copyright relations with other countries. As an example, a movie published in Iran can be copied and performed in the United States without being considered infringement.

WIPO

The World Intellectual Property Organization (WIPO) works to ensure international protection for intellectual property.

International movie star Javier Bardem speaks about copyright and the film industry at a WIPO conference.

The organization helps creators gain protection for their works outside of their native countries. This is accomplished through intellectual-property treaties and global registration systems for trademarks and patents. WIPO also works to enforce existing agreements.

In particular, WIPO is involved in the effort to develop international standards for copyright protection in cyberspace.

WIPO'S WORK

WIPO promotes human creativity through worldwide cooperation. The organization was established in 1970 and became an agency of the United Nations in 1974. It is headquartered in Geneva, Switzerland, and features 188 member states.[5] Increasing global trade and rapid changes in technology have provided opportunities for WIPO to negotiate treaties, provide legal and technical assistance, and train policymakers in ways to protect intellectual property.

In 2008, WIPO adopted a Strategic Realignment Program in response to the ever-growing complexities of intellectual property. The program addressed the challenges the organization faced in terms of evolving technology, globalization, and market demands. The ultimate goal was "encouraging creativity and innovation in all countries."[6]

It administers Internet treaties that ensure copyright owners are protected when their works are posted online. It also gives countries flexibility in setting up exceptions or limitations to Internet rights. Such exceptions include uses of materials for education and research or to benefit people with disabilities.

INTERNATIONAL COPYRIGHT AGREEMENTS

With no universal copyright law among nations, international conventions and treaties have some benefits and some drawbacks. One benefit is that they can address the differences among nations' copyright laws. For example, international conventions can help resolve issues that arise from differences in the duration of copyright protection.

On the other hand, one drawback is that it is difficult to pursue legal action against copyright infringement in a foreign country.

WIPO Director General Kamil Idris, *left*, and Swiss Minister of Justice and Police Christoph Blocher, *right*, cooperate in the global copyright arena.

Under the Berne Convention, an infringement lawsuit is tried in the courts of the country in which the infringement occurred and prosecuted according to that country's laws. Some people argue this is a hardship for foreign copyright owners whose works have been infringed.

With its complexities and inconsistencies, international copyright issues can draw some criticism. Some critics also question whether US copyright law is living up to its intended purposes on a national level.

CHAPTER 9

WHAT'S WRONG WITH COPYRIGHTS?

The classic holiday movie *It's a Wonderful Life* was made in 1946. At that time, US copyright protection lasted 28 years and could be renewed for another 28 years. But Republic Pictures, the copyright owner, accidentally neglected to renew *It's a Wonderful Life* in 1974. The film entered the public domain. Television networks were free to show it, which they did—over and over—during the holidays in the late 1970s and 1980s. The movie gained more popularity than when it was first released.

The movie was based on a short story called "The Greatest Gift" by Phillip Van Doren Stern. Republic Pictures owned and still maintained the copyright to the original story. This allowed Republic Pictures to reclaim copyright protection for the movie. The argument was that the film was a derivative work based on Stern's short story and therefore protected under the story's copyright. The Supreme Court case of *Stewart v. Abend* (1990) supported this claim.

It's a Wonderful Life came in and out of the public domain, prompting some to question the copyright system.

It's a Wonderful Life was removed from the public domain. The movie could no longer be shown without permission and a license fee. NBC signed a contract with Republic Pictures to broadcast *It's a Wonderful Life* only a few times a year. Paramount Pictures acquired Republic Pictures in 1999. Then, in 2013, Paramount blocked another company's plans to make a sequel.

Removing *It's a Wonderful Life* from the public domain turned out to be a complicated decision. On one hand, supporters claimed it protected the rights of a short story writer. On the other hand, opponents felt the decision stifled the creative efforts of those who wanted to build on a popular film.

❝Just like that, the era of 'It's a Wonderful Life' TV marathons was over, for better or worse.❞ [2]

—*Plagiarism Today*, on the reinstating of the film's copyright

Either way, *It's a Wonderful Life* serves as a controversial example of the many questions critics pose about current copyright law.

HAS COPYRIGHT LAW LOST SIGHT OF ITS PURPOSE?

Some people feel copyright law has lost sight of its intended purpose—to promote the progress of creative expression. Actions or laws that seemingly work against the progress of creative expression are sometimes called "copywrongs."[1]

In particular, many critics believe the extension of copyright protection and the resulting limitation of the public domain are major flaws in current copyright law. They also point to the increasing number of orphan works as another tragic consequence.

Critics emphasize that "copywrongs" impede the creative progress and keep works locked up from public use.

The Center for the Study of the Public Domain raises this question: "At what point in time in the life of a work do we believe that a copyright holder should no longer have a unilateral veto over those who wish to build on a work?"[3] After all, critics claim, extending copyright disrupts the design of the system: copyright encourages the creation of new works, protects those works for a time, and then encourages the creation of new works once the

> **❝**Only one thing is impossible for God: to find any sense in any copyright law on the planet. **❞**[4]
> —Mark Twain, author and humorist

Few people are willing to risk the time or money on legal procedures for copyright matters.

originals enter the public domain. To keep extending the term length is to alter the intended purpose.

IS THE LEGAL PROCESS TOO COMPLICATED?

Because copyright laws and fair use guidelines are sometimes unclear, many copyright issues must be determined in court on a case-by-case basis. But critics argue the legal process is a risky business for everyone involved.

Defending a copyright in court can be a financial burden for some copyright owners. A copyright owner may pursue an infringement case only to find it judged fair use. Or a creator may defend a work that ends up being judged a derivative of another copyrighted work. In addition, if a copyright holder claims infringement but a court determines the case to be unwarranted, the holder may face penalties. With such uncertainty and financial risk, copyright owners may be reluctant to turn to the legal system.

The legal process can also be a financial burden for individuals using copyrighted material. Worried about infringement lawsuits, some users pass up opportunities to legitimately and fairly use copyrighted works. Or when faced with an infringement claim, some users choose to cease and desist rather than go to court—even though a decision might have been in their favor. Again, the uncertainty and costs are significant disadvantages.

IS US COPYRIGHT LAW OUTDATED?

Although copyright law has been revised and updated several times, critics argue more changes are needed, especially for digital works. The DMCA was intended to be the first step in an ongoing reform process, yet it became a target of criticism from many directions.

Critics say the act quickly became obsolete and raised as many legal questions as it

WHAT TO DO ABOUT THE DMCA

The DMCA was one of the most controversial copyright laws in history. The intention of the law—to move the nation's copyright law into the digital age—was thought to be good. But the effects, according to one critic, were "the mother lode of unintended consequences."[5] For example, one of its restrictions on digital rights management made it potentially illegal to make repairs on some cars or unlock cell phones.

A rule-making process that takes place every three years allows copyright users to request exemptions. In 2015, the Electronic Frontier Foundation (EFF) successfully argued and won several exemptions from the DMCA regarding such matters as repair of car software and mobile devices. But critics see the need for many additional reforms.

has answered. The Electronic Frontier Foundation (EFF) calls itself the leading nonprofit organization defending civil liberties in the digital world. The EFF has called the DMCA "a serious threat that jeopardizes fair use, impedes competition and innovation, chills free expression, and scientific research and interferes with computer intrusion laws."[6]

IS THE US COPYRIGHT OFFICE OUTDATED?

The US Copyright Office is part of the Library of Congress, which controls the Copyright Office's budget and approves its policies. The Copyright Office lacks the resources to update its technology. Delays frustrate people seeking permission to use works. And even though copyright registration is beneficial, some creators never register their works because the outdated procedure is time-consuming.

In response to critiques, Maria Pallante, head of

THE NEXT GENERATION COPYRIGHT ACT

Maria Pallante was appointed US Register of Copyrights in 2011, and she began to prepare the Copyright Office for the future. Her first step was a two-year evaluation of current problems, which included public meetings in major US cities. The next step was to promote a comprehensive congressional review of US copyright law.

Pallante created programs to improve understanding of current copyright law. These included a lecture series for copyright experts and a research program for law schools. Pallante also submitted to Congress policy studies that supported revision of copyright law for the future. She urged Congress to "think big" and create the next generation copyright.[7]

the Copyright Office, has consistently argued in favor of an independent office with updated technology that could efficiently meet the needs of the trillion-dollar US copyright industry. Pending legislation was expected to address the issues by 2017.

WHAT CAN BE DONE?

With so many questions about the copyright system, many people are searching for answers and solutions. One proposed remedy is education. Organizations such as the EFF provide tips for teachers wishing to give students a better understanding of copyright.

Alternative solutions to copyright reform include a licensing program that enables copyright owners to allow specific uses of their works. For instance, through Creative Commons, a creator can grant free licenses that allow others to use a copyrighted work without individual permission or fees.

Most people want a copyright law that is easily understood and that balances the interests of both creators and the public. Representing the rights of creators, the Authors Alliance proposed changes that would help authors make their works more accessible, clarify fair use, limit copyright protection, and make it easier to enforce infringement claims. Public interest groups have expressed concerns that lobbying and financial considerations—rather than the general good of the public—are influencing copyright reform. They have petitioned policymakers to address the issues of long copyright terms and to enact sensible reforms.

Both supporters and critics of copyright law agree that reform is needed, but they understand it will require a huge effort. Revisions to copyright law have historically required years of debate in Congress. The last major revision of copyright law began in the late 1950s and did not go into effect until 1978.

But an initial plan for new reform was set in motion in 2013. A House of Representatives subcommittee began hearings to consider Pallante's recommendations. In a speech delivered to Columbia Law School that year, Pallante said, "The next great copyright act is as possible as it is exciting. Most importantly, it would serve the public interest."[9]

Maria Pallante calls for reform of the Copyright Office she leads.

ESSENTIAL FACTS

MAJOR EVENTS

» In 1790, Congress passed the first US copyright law.

» In 1976, a major revision of US copyright law lengthened copyright protection and established guidelines for fair use of copyrighted works.

» In 1998, the Sonny Bono Copyright Extension Act extended the terms of almost all existing US copyrights for 20 years.

» In 2000, the Digital Millennium Copyright Act attempted to move US copyright law into the digital age.

KEY PLAYERS

» The US Copyright Office is a department of the Library of Congress that issues copyrights and maintains a database of copyrighted works and ownership information.

» The World Intellectual Property Organization is an agency of the United Nations that works to ensure international protection for industrial property and copyrighted materials.

» Creative Commons is an organization that creates licenses to enable the sharing of copyrighted works.

IMPACT ON SOCIETY

The primary purpose of US copyright law is to encourage the growth of human knowledge by protecting creative efforts. The public benefits from copyrighted works as well as from the transformations of works made possible by the public domain. Fair use limits copyright protection for purposes of criticism, comment, news reporting, teaching, or research. Through international treaties and conventions, many countries offer protection to foreign works. Copyright laws are extremely complex, and both supporters and critics agree that reform is needed. Government and private organizations seek solutions to the issues of copyright protection in the digital age.

QUOTE

"Everyone has the right to the protection of the moral and material interests resulting from any scientific, literary, or artistic production of which he is the author."

—*United Nations, Universal Declaration of Human Rights*

GLOSSARY

CEASE AND DESIST LETTER
A document telling an individual or business to stop unlawful activity and not take it up again.

COPYRIGHT
The right to control the production and sale of a creative work.

DIGITIZE
To put information into digital form.

DOWNLOAD
To copy data from one computer system to another over the Internet.

EXCLUSIVE RIGHTS
Rights that can be controlled by a single individual.

LIABLE
To be bound or responsible according to law.

LICENSE

To give permission for something to be used, often in exchange for payment.

PLAGIARISM

The act of copying and claiming another person's words or ideas as your own.

ROYALTY

A share of money generated by sales of a work.

UNCONSTITUTIONAL

Being inconsistent with the constitution of a state or society.

ADDITIONAL RESOURCES

SELECTED BIBLIOGRAPHY

"Copyright Law of the United States of America." *US Copyright Office*. US Copyright Office, n.d. Web. 1 Jan. 2016.

Fishman, Stephen. *The Copyright Handbook*. Berkeley, CA: Nolo, 2014. Print.

Simpson, Carol. *Copyright for Schools*. Worthington, OH: Linworth, 2001. Print.

FURTHER READINGS

Doctorow, Cory. *Content: Selected Essays on Technology, Creativity, Copyright, and the Future of the Future*. San Francisco: Tachyon, 2008. Print.

Gilmore, Barry. *Plagiarism: A How-Not-to Guide for Students*. Portsmouth, NH: Heinemann, 2009. Print.

Hobbs, Renee. *Copyright Clarity: How Fair Use Supports Digital Learning*. Thousand Oaks, CA: Corwin, 2010. Print.

WEBSITES

To learn more about Essential Library of the Information Age, visit **booklinks.abdopublishing.com**. These links are routinely monitored and updated to provide the most current information available.

FOR MORE INFORMATION

For more information on this subject, contact or visit the following organizations:

Center for the Study of the Public Domain

Duke University Law School
210 Science Drive
Box 90360
Durham, NC 27708-0360
919-613-7003
http://web.law.duke.edu/cspd/

The Center for the Study of the Public Domain promotes research and scholarship on the contributions of the public domain to intellectual property. It promotes awareness about the balance needed in the intellectual property system.

US Copyright Office

101 Independence Avenue SE
Washington, DC 20559-6000
202-707-3000
https://www.copyright.gov

The US Copyright Office registers copyrights and maintains the world's largest copyright database. It provides copyright information to the public and carries out law and policy functions for Congress.

SOURCE NOTES

CHAPTER 1. PROTECTING CREATIVE EFFORTS

1. Stelios Phili. "Robin Thicke on That Banned Video, Collaborating with 2 Chainz and Kendrick Lamar, and His New Film." *GQ*. Condé Nast, 6 May 2013. Web. 24 Feb. 2016.

2. "Jury Finds Pharrell, Thicke Copied Marvin Gaye Song for 'Blurred Lines.'" *Chicago Tribune*. Tribune Publishing Company, 11 Mar. 2015. Web. 24 Feb. 2016.

3. Jessica Goodman. "Pharrell Slams 'Blurred Lines' Verdict." *Huffington Post*. TheHuffingtonPost.com, 3 Mar. 2015. Web. 24 Feb. 2016.

4. Kenneth D. Crews. *Copyright Law for Librarians and Educators: Creative Strategies and Practical Solutions*. American Library Association, 2012. Google Books. Web. 24 Feb. 2016.

5. "*Sony BMG Music Entertainment v. Tenenbaum*. 12-2146 (1st Cir. 2013)." *Justia*. Justia, 29 Oct. 2015. Web. 24 Feb. 2016.

6. Denise Lavoie. "Court Reinstates $675,000 Damages for Downloading." *Seattle Times*. Seattle Times Company, 19 Sept. 2011. Web. 24 Feb. 2016.

7. Denise Lavoie. "Jury Orders Student to Pay $675,000 for Illegally Downloading Music." *ABC News*. ABC News Internet Ventures, 25 June 2013. Web. 24 Feb. 2016.

8. Bob Greene. "Irving Berlin's Gift of 'God Bless America.'" *CNN*. Turner Broadcasting System, 12 Dec. 2011. Web. 24 Feb. 2016.

CHAPTER 2. HOW COPYRIGHT WORKS

1. James Boyle. *The Public Domain: Enclosing the Commons of the Mind*. New Haven, CT: Yale UP, 2008. Print. 14.

2. "General Guide to the Copyright Act of 1976." *USCO*. USCO, Sept. 1977. Web. 24 Feb. 2016.

CHAPTER 3. USING COPYRIGHTED MATERIAL

1. "*Warner Bros. Entertainment Inc. v. RDR Books*. 575 F. Supp. 2d 513 (2008)." *USCO*. USCO, n.d. Web. 24 Feb. 2016.

2. "*Feist Publications, Inc. v. Rural Telephone Service Co.*, 499 US 340, 349 (1991)." *FindLaw*. FindLaw, n.d. Web. 24 Feb. 2016.

3. Tonya Marie Evans and Susan Borden Evans. *Literary Law Guide for Authors*. Philadelphia: FYOS Entertainment, 2003. Print. 51.

4. "Dan Brown Wins 'Da Vinci' Battle." *CNN*. Turner Broadcasting System, 7 Apr. 2006. Web. 24 Feb. 2016.

5. "*Warner Bros. Entertainment Inc. v. RDR Books*. 575 F. Supp. 2d 513 (2008)." *USCO*. USCO, n.d. Web. 24 Feb. 2016.

6. "*Princeton University Press v. Michigan Document Services*. 99 F.3rd 1381 (1996)." *Cornell University Law School*. Cornell University, n.d. Web. 24 Feb. 2016.

CHAPTER 4. PUBLIC DOMAIN

1. Eugene Volokh. "Monkey See, Monkey Sue Is Not Good Law." *Washington Post*. Washington Post, 16 Nov. 2015. Web. 24 Feb. 2016.

2. Derek Khanna. "50 Disney Movies Based on the Public Domain." *Forbes*. Forbes, 3 Feb. 2014. Web. 24 Feb. 2016.

3. Corynne McSherry. "The Orphan Works Problem: Time to Fix It." *Electronic Frontier Foundation*. Electronic Frontier Foundation, 4 Feb. 2013. Web. 24 Feb. 2016.

4. "Orphan Works." *USCO*. USCO, n.d. Web. 24 Feb. 2016.

5. Jennifer Jenkins. "'Til the End of Eternity?" *Huffington Post*. TheHuffingtonPost.com, 3 Oct. 2012. Web. 24 Feb. 2016.

6. Timothy B. Lee. "15 Years Ago, Congress Kept Mickey Mouse out of the Public Domain. Will They Do It Again?" *Washington Post*. Washington Post, 25 Oct. 2013. Web. 24 Feb. 2016.

CHAPTER 5. INTELLECTUAL PROPERTY

1. "What Is Intellectual Property?" *WIPO*. WIPO, n.d. Web. 24 Feb. 2016.

2. "The Universal Declaration of Human Rights." *United Nations*. United Nations, n.d. Web. 24 Feb. 2016.

3. "Michael Jordan Awarded $8.9M for Store's Use of Image." *USA Today*. USA Today, 21 Aug. 2015. Web. 24 Feb. 2016.

4. "About Piracy." *RIAA*. RIAA, 2016. Web. 24 Feb. 2016.

5. Kim Jansen. "Jordan Says, 'It Was Never about the Money' after $8.9M Jury Award." *Chicago Tribune*. Tribune Publishing Company, 21 Aug. 2015. Web. 24 Feb. 2016.

CHAPTER 6. COPYRIGHTS AND SCHOOLS

1. Linda Starr. "Applying Fair Use to New Technologies." *Education World*. Education World, 25 May 2010. Web. 24 Feb. 2016.

CHAPTER 7. COPYRIGHTS IN THE DIGITAL AGE

1. "Authors Guild v. Google." *Authors Guild*. Authors Guild, n.d. Web. 24 Feb. 2016.

2. Corynne McSherry. "Big Win for Fair Use in Google Books Lawsuit." *Electronic Frontier Foundation*. Electronic Frontier Foundation, 16 Oct. 2015. Web. 24 Feb. 2016.

3. "Executive Summary Digital Millennium Copyright Act." *USCO*. USCO, n.d. Web. 24 Feb. 2016.

4. Gerhard Peters and John T. Woolley. "William J. Clinton: Statement on Signing the Digital Millennium Copyright Act." *The American Presidency Project*. Gerhard Peters and John T. Woolley—The American Presidency Project, 28 Oct. 1998. Web. 24 Feb. 2016.

5. Sarah Mitroff and Matthew Moskovciak. "6 Things to Consider When Choosing a Streaming-Music Subscription." *CNET*. CBS Interactive, 25 Sept. 2015. Web. 24 Feb. 2016.

6. Tom Lamont. "Napster: the Day the Music Was Set Free." *The Guardian*. Guardian News and Media Limited, 23 Feb. 2013. Web. 24 Feb. 2016.

7. "Napster to Start Screening Copyrighted Material." *CNN*. Turner Broadcasting System, 2 Mar. 2001. 24 Feb. 2016.

CHAPTER 8. GLOBAL COPYRIGHT ISSUES

1. Andrew Albanese "What Does *Kirtsaeng v. Wiley* Mean for the Industry?" *Publishers Weekly*. PWxyz, 23 Mar. 2013. Web. 24 Feb. 2016.

2. Joint Information Systems Committee. "Disabled Learners Celebrate Changes to Copyright Law." *Jisc*. Jisc, 2 June 2014. Web. 24 Feb. 2016.

3. "WIPO-administered Treaties." *WIPO*. WIPO, n.d. Web. 24 Feb. 2016.

4. Orrin G. Hatch. "Better Late Than Never: Implementation of the 1886 Berne Convention." *Cornell International Law Journal*. Cornell University, 1989. Web. 24 Feb. 2016.

5. "What Is Intellectual Property?" *WIPO*. WIPO, n.d. Web. 24 Feb. 2016.

6. "WIPO Strategic Realignment Program." *WIPO*. WIPO, n.d. Web. 24 Feb. 2016.

CHAPTER 9. WHAT'S WRONG WITH COPYRIGHTS?

1. James Surowiecki. "Righting Copywrongs." *New Yorker*. Condé Nast, 21 Jan. 2002. Web. 24 Feb. 2016.

2. Jonathan Bailey. "It's a Wonderful (Copyright) Life." *Plagiarism Today*. Jonathan Bailey, 5 Dec. 2013. Web. 24 Feb. 2016.

3. "Public Domain Day 2015." *Center for the Study of the Public Domain*. Center for the Study of the Public Domain, 1 Jan. 2015. Web. 24 Feb. 2016.

4. Mark Twain. *Mark Twain's Notebook*. New York: Harper & Brothers, 1935. Print. 381.

5. George Sandoval. "The Head of the Copyright Office Says the Law Is Broken—But Can She Fix It in Time?" *Verge*. Vox Media, 20 March 2013. Web. 24 Feb. 2016.

6. "Digital Millennium Copyright Act." *EFF*. EFF, n.d. Web. 24 Feb. 2016.

7. "The Next Great Copyright Act." *USCO*. USCO, 19 Mar. 2013. Web. 24 Feb. 2016.

8. "What Is Creative Commons?" *Creative Commons*. Creative Commons, n.d. Web. 24 Feb. 2016.

9. "The Next Great Copyright Act". *USCO*. USCO, 19 Mar. 2013. Web. 24 Feb. 2016.

INDEX

adaptation, 23–24, 44–45

A&M Records, Inc. v. Napster, Inc.,
   77, 79

Authors Guild v. Google, 68, 70

A.V. v. iParadigms, L.L.C., 58, 60–61

Baraban, Joe, 38

Batmobile, 24–26

Berlin, Irving, 15

Berne Convention, 85–86, 89

"Blurred Lines," 4, 6, 10, 13

Brown, Dan, 34–35

caching, 73

Center for the Study of the Public
   Domain, 46, 93

Church Picnic, 36–37

Congress, 21, 26, 43, 46, 48, 50, 72,
   77, 86, 96, 98

Constitution, 8, 50, 54

content ownership, 7, 17

copyright
   extension, 46–49, 85, 92
   notice, 21, 86
   registration, 21–22, 86, 87, 96
   symbol, 21

Copyright Act of 1976, 26, 30, 63,
   67, 76

Copyright Office, 21, 22, 26, 42, 46,
   77, 96–97

copywrongs, 92

Creative Commons, 97

Da Vinci Code, The, 34–35

DC Comics v. Towle, 25–26

derivative work, 24–26, 36, 76, 90

Digital Millennium Copyright Act
   (DMCA), 72–74, 95–96

Dominick's Finer Foods, 55–57

Eldred v. Ashcroft, 48

Electronic Frontier Foundation
   (EFF), 95, 96

fair use, 27, 28, 30–31, 32–33, 36, 38,
   60–67, 70, 72, 73, 74–75, 76, 83,
   94, 96, 98

Fanning, Shawn, 78–79

four factors, 32–33, 36, 60, 62, 75–76

Gaye, Marvin, 4, 6

Girl Scouts, 10–11, 15

Golan v. Holder, 43

Google Books, 68, 70

Harry Potter series, 28, 30, 32–33, 36

Holy Blood and the Holy Grail, The,
   34–35

infringement, 4, 6, 10, 13, 17, 25–26,
   28–32, 34–35, 37, 38, 43, 46, 53,
   67, 68, 72–74, 76, 78–79, 80, 86,
   88–89, 94–95, 98

intellectual property, 49, 50–57, 62,
   68, 86–88

Internet, 23, 60, 67, 70, 72–77, 97

Internet service provider (ISP),
   72–73

It's a Wonderful Life, 90, 92

Jordan, Michael, 55–57

Kirtsaeng v. John Wiley & Sons, Inc.,
   80, 82

Library of Congress, 21, 46, 96
licensing, 10, 15, 37, 38, 82, 92, 97

Napster, 77, 78–79
Naruto, 40, 42

orphan works, 45–46, 92

Pallante, Maria, 96, 97, 98
Parker, Sean, 78–79
parody, 30, 31
patent, 50, 52–53, 83, 87
permission, 18, 23, 24, 27, 30, 31, 32, 37, 42, 55, 58, 62, 64–65, 67, 68, 72, 74–75, 77, 80, 82, 83, 92, 96, 97
persona, 55–57
plagiarism, 58, 60–61, 62
public domain, 38, 40–49, 62, 70, 72, 77, 85, 90, 92, 94, 97

Ringgold, Faith, 36–37
Rowling, J. K., 28, 36

safe harbor provision, 72–73
Slater, David, 40, 42
Sonny Bono Copyright Term Extension Act of 1998, 48
students, 12, 13, 18, 30, 58–67, 80, 97
Supreme Court, 43, 48, 82, 90

takedown notice, 74
TEACH Act of 2002, 67
teachers, 58, 60, 63–67, 97
Tenenbaum, Joel, 13–17, 76
Thicke, Robin, 4, 6
Titanic, 24
Towle, Mark, 24–26

trademark, 50, 52, 53–55, 57, 61, 62, 83, 87
Turnitin, 58, 60–61

United Kingdom, 83
United Nations Educational, Scientific and Cultural Organization, 85
US Patent and Trademark Office (USPTO), 52

Vander Ark, Steven, 28, 30, 36

Warner Brothers Entertainment, Inc. v. RDR Books, 28, 32
Washington, George, 8, 12
Williams, Pharrell, 4, 6
work for hire, 23
World Intellectual Property Organization (WIPO), 86–88

ABOUT THE AUTHOR

Carolee Laine is an educator and children's writer. She has written social studies textbooks and other educational materials as well as passages for statewide assessments. She enjoys learning through researching and writing nonfiction books for young readers. Laine lives in the Chicago suburbs.

ABOUT THE CONSULTANT

Brandy Karl is an attorney and the copyright officer for the Pennsylvania State University Libraries. She advises on copyright matters and serves as an expert in the university community for copyright and fair use questions. She helps faculty, staff, and students understand how copyright affects their work as well as how they can make informed decisions in the use and creation of copyrighted works.